I0390986

NEW FOUNDATIONS

By Alan Porter

ISBN 978-1-326-85348-8

'New Foundations' was written in early 2006. No word, phrase or policy has been altered. These words have only now been placed in the public domain. Now is the time and place for this new thinking to be heard and read.

The emblem for a new flag which is on the front of the book symbolises the diverse cultures we have in our country today. By harnessing this energy of diverse cultures, together we can create a better society for everyone.

These thoughts are the seeds to a new way of thinking; driven by the belief that we are all capable of achieving greater goals for ourselves which will benefit everyone. These ideas are just the bones that can be assembled into a greater body for good. The flesh will be added by the extension of further thoughts; resulting in actions which can bring about results.

We have got to forge a new direction built on spiritual values, principles and morals. This will cement the new building blocks which will be the *NEW FOUNDATIONS*.

A Change of Direction Brought About by a Consensus of Thoughts That Can Benefit Everyone

All religions and faiths have one thing in common, they are all spiritual people acting, thinking, and believing, with the same spiritual energy.

This is the link, which will be forged into uniting all nations and cultures. No longer will divisions of religion and ideology, prevent humankind from fusing their spiritual energy towards those who have so little in life.

Therefore, the rich will help the poor; the strong will help the weak. Nations will help to build new nations. The gifted will give to those who wish to aspire to self-improvement. Indeed, the tide will turn when human kindness will break down every barrier that man has constructed. This ripple of change will grow into a wave, which will eventually engulf everyone. Good will overcome any evil intent.

These new foundations permeating society will embody the principle that the spiritual power of women is equal to that of men. All decisions taken at every level of government office must have an equal proportion of women to men. In every sphere of thinking where new ideas will abound, women will play an equal and active part to men. This will result in bringing about a new balance and harmony to the world that has never been seen before.

It is now time to have a new government of unity that embraces women to share equally with men. A new vision for the future is required; a new direction which will bring change for the benefit of all, resulting in a new sense of hope, which will be combined with meaning and purpose to life itself.

A building is only as secure, solid and strong as the foundation that it is built on. Therefore, strong foundations have to be laid, which will have all of its corners secured on a philosophy or way of thinking, that is anchored with spiritual values that accommodate religions and faiths in a way of uniting them to a common goal. The philosophy that inspires all can unite all. The foundation of core beliefs must stand for any new generation that aspires to live a life seeking peace, not conflict.

Certainly, fulfilment rather than having any regrets is paramount. Therefore, personal fulfilment combined with love for others is the perfect recipe to having a happier life. This foundation must endorse the whole of society having an equal opportunity from whatever circumstances they find themselves in.

The three major political parties in the United Kingdom are now past their sell-by date. In England they have served a menu of politics that has now become totally unpalatable. The public has been fed this boring and stale diet for far too long now. It is their political thoughts and persuasions that have created a perpetual pattern of the 'blind leading the blind.'

With a lack of vision and planning, which has pervaded each political party's ideology, we have been left with a legacy of apathy and disillusionment for this present young generation. This continuing feeling of hopelessness for the future is contaminating every age group. We seem to be in a sea of becalmed water, where the never-ending corrosive decisions continue to make the very fabric of our country look worn and threadbare.

We will help to create a society that does not place material wealth as the pinnacle of achievement, or place false idolatry of innocuous celebrities, who represent false gods to the young. We will help to resurrect the doctrine made famous by the late President John. F. Kennedy who said, "Do not ask what your government can do for you, but ask what can you do for your country."

A new democracy is required to this great country of ours; a new and fresh beginning which can bring hope, meaning, and purpose to all our lives. We have to change *now* in order to prevent any more of our young ones taking their gifts, talents, and abilities to distant shores.

A unification of ideas and policies can bring together the energy and diverse talents that we possess as a nation. The ideologies and dogmas that are prevalent today, who's roots have stunted the growth, aspirations and visions of a society, have deteriorated metaphorically into a garden that is dying, with so many weeds of its own making, suffocating any life that is left in it.

Three forums, or assemblies, embracing individuals that represent all spectrums of society, would be able to express and evaluate new ideas and visions that are proposed in order to bring changes for the better of society. Such a new democracy will eliminate the divisive aspects of parties sitting in opposing directions, allowing changes for the better to be more easily and effectively implemented.

Unifying all these various qualities, intellect, imagination, ideals, and aspirations, will provide the momentum for spiritual energy to take place, promoting only the desire to do good for each other. This will, in turn, set the example for everyone to think of others, thereby helping others, in order to help your self. This is now the time to fuse such energies together. We do not have time to proceed any further down this present road of destruction, where policy, and decisions are, in truth, not been taken by consensus of the people. Only a small majority of the electorate are really endorsing such decisions, because most people are so disillusioned with the political choice on the menu, they are not even bothering with their 'right to vote'. Therefore, new ingredients are required in order to offer a more appealing menu. So, with a foundation in place, we need to build on this foundation with new, strong, solid building blocks.

The New Building Blocks

The first assembly, or forum, will be of young people from the age of 23 years through to the age of 35 years, consisting equally of males and females. Two (one man, one woman) would be elected from each constituency. They would need to have fresh, exciting, and effective ideas and visions of what they believe will bring about a better society. They would need the approval of their constituency to implement these new ideas, in order to replace what is in place at present. With this mandate of their constituency, they would serve a term of four years. After this term, elections would take place again.

This forum would be the hub of nurturing new ideas and bringing them to fruition, in order to improve the present stagnation of our society. Those who have a clear insight into what is required to bring improvement to society, and an art of oratory that encompasses the skill of communication, will be needed in order to form an inner cabinet and leadership, which will be required to make sure such ideas and visions, steer this society in the right direction.

This first forum would have power; for once they have formulated a good idea they would have to seek support from the higher forum. If that support added enough votes, which then gave a majority of votes between the two forums, then this would be presented to the country as an important issue that the people would then vote on. This would be decided by the consensus of the people. We could now see democracy working for the common good of all, instead of the privileged few.

The second forum would be from the age of 35 years until whatever age permits a delegate of people to continue until they feel they have nothing else to give. The same selection process would operate with this forum as the first. Therefore, there would be equal numbers of men and women, elected to four-year periods, and they would submit to the wishes and needs of their constituency. Again, their ideas and plans would have to gain votes from the first forum, giving a majority vote between the two forums. This format allows the young to possess power like never before, as their new ideas, if better than the old, would be implemented with consensus of the majority.

Moreover, there would be a third forum, based on those who have been leaders of industry and other fields. These would be people who have seen the adversities of life, and overcome their trials. These would be men and women whose characters have been shaped by their life experiences. They would all bring valuable experience, wisdom, and knowledge of this university of living. This forum would be one to have and hear their thoughts of new ideas, so long as they believed these were for the good of all.

However, they would not have the power to block, but they would be given the opportunity of persuasion, so long as their argument is based on knowledge and wisdom. It would be taken into account that they deserve respect, as they would be high achievers in their specialised field. Therefore, the relevant people would listen and think about their views, if decisions are to be made. The people would also elect this third forum on a four-year cycle.

For all constituencies, at local levels they could operate the same format, so that they could decide how their local community could develop, and how they wanted their town, and neighbourhood to operate. There would be many areas where the government would not stamp the same for all.

Life is about diversity; different cultures, different faiths, and beliefs. We would inspire and encourage young people that they have the capabilities to qualify for far greater things in this life. At the moment finance, poor parenting, poor education and a distinct lack of understanding to the meaning of life still exists. We would open a new door of new thinking for the young.

Harness this energy, and we will have a power that is far greater than the destructive force created by man and the nuclear power, that could condemn us to the end of life as we know it on the earth plane.

By looking at different aspects of society, such as taxation, education, health, industry etc., it is possible to see how plausible it can be to create a more positive and brighter future for everyone.

Pensions

Pensions have to be the sole responsibility of the government. Company pensions have proved that they cannot supply the expectations that were given to their employees in the first place. Companies cannot guarantee pensions being there years ahead, when they themselves may not be successful to still be trading.

We have to give a pension that is free of any monetary contributions, and can provide a good home and warmth for everyone. Therefore, everyone would be entitled to adequate allowances, showing equality to our society. We cannot afford to have divides in society. Failure to do so would result in a total breakdown in society, where anarchy would reign.

The superficial thinking that we can all pay our way into providing our own pension is a fallacy, when we all find ourselves in different circumstances. So many in this debt-ridden society cannot even pay their own way in the short-term; never mind thinking about saving for their pension. Indeed, many people are trying their best just to be financially solvent.

The government must relieve industry of being the guardians to pension funds. By governing in a proper manner, industry would have more time, energy, and capital, to compete more efficiently and effectively.

Change in how we live, act, and think, is paramount to our future. However, we cannot just accept that the government can just turn on a tap to fund everything adequately. We all need to be united and believe that we all play a part individually.

Taxation

Taxation equals the funding of government that allows them to continue fuelling this mammoth train that carries so many unwanted carriages. We are continually pulling a greater weight, or burden, that is chained to an out-dated policy of economic growth. We can eliminate so many of these carriages, making life much easier.

Through the following aspects of government the pieces of change will emerge. We can create a financial figure, which allows those, whether they are single, or a family, to lead a life with a comfortable home and basic needs, without having to pay tax. If others would like to have more material possessions, then taxes will be placed on those items and products accordingly. Luxury goods will be higher in taxes. We need to get away from the myth that material possessions bring happiness. Indeed, the opposite could be true if they bring debt and ill health, due to stress.

The concept of 'off-shore' accounts and 'clever' accounting should be wholly discouraged and stopped. This would result in closing the large hole created by the black market of tax avoidance. Moreover, the majority go down this particular road because of our present tax system that stifles those who want their families to have more. The whole system encourages individuals to spend a live of hedonism, because it is fuelled by economic growth. Consequently, we live in a society that judges an individual's success by the amount of material wealth and status symbols that they possess. Such a system is geared up for whom? In short, the rich get richer and the poor become poorer. We have to look at how we are living, as the actions of now, bring our tomorrow.

Elimination of inheritance tax is just one of many changes required. As a consequence of the surreal times that we are living in, we are witnessing the hard work of many evaporating. Houses are becoming further out of reach for many, and many others are losing their houses due to repossessions. This means that many are not able to leave homes for their children. Furthermore, many have to sell their houses to finance an elderly parent entering a care home. Such ones would be refunded and the practice would cease immediately.

Housing

Addressing the housing problem is probably one of the most important issues facing us. Providing comfortable homes for the young at affordable prices is paramount to solving so many of today's self-made problems. The answer is changing the culture that a home is about making money; this is not so. We need to take the financial profit out of building houses. The purpose of a home is to provide the necessary facilities that enable a person, or family, to live in a happy and harmonious environment. This allows the family unit to create a better life for all. The profit is then found in society as less homes experience break-up etc.

We need to build homes that can be constructed in weeks and days, built in sections of materials that could even give the impression that it was built with bricks. This is not only feasible and practical; it is not even a new idea.

Land could be acquired that would not have this idea of profit attached to it, and the government could be the source to provide the money at affordable loans over a lifetime. People could still move and exchanges could be made. However, the idea of profiting out of someone else's misfortune of not having a home will finish.

Once this plan is put into action we would see a dramatic change in house prices. Today's market is fuelling the crisis, which is motivating so many of our young to move abroad purely because homes are cheaper.

Change is required now. We are already at the time of two minutes to midnight; there is not much time left to avoid and stop the present meltdown of our society.

Industry

We have to create a new climate and policy regarding industry, and what industry is to contribute to our society. At the moment so much bureaucracy and red tape hold industry and small businesses back. Most of these new regulations are made not by ourselves, but by the E.U. This must cease forthwith and many such rules and regulations must be rescinded. We need to remove the fallacy that one rule suits all, that one particular economic model suits all other countries; it does not and never will. It is vital that we have complete freedom to have an economy that can be changed at our own will, when climates of business and trade change, so will we. Just like a sailing ship, you can change course or adapt your sails to suit all possibilities of weather conditions.

We should question the myth that a growing economy is right or good for a country. A growing economy is more than likely to be fuelled by consumers purchasing more material goods. One can see society as it is, and question the right and wrongs of purchasing more material wants, rather than necessities.

There needs to be more incentives for speculative ideas that can benefit the needs of society. There should be greater encouragement for those who try to produce items for the future. Furthermore, there needs to be further tax breaks for those who want to make further investments in their company.

There should be greater financial help and advice for those trying to establish their own business. This would herald a new era when the inventor and innovator would become a modern-day hero. They would be recognised for the good that increased wealth would be apportioned out far more equally.

For those that seek tax havens and offshore accounts, that is fine. However, they forfeit their citizenship and right to employ their skills in this country. Moreover, 'clever' accounting will not be tolerated. For those who create for themselves extreme amounts of money compared to the majority of others, an option will be given to them. They could spend a large amount of their income on worthwhile needs and causes in society rather than paying further taxation.

For instance, one could have a hospital unit named after them, when funded by an excess of their wealth. This could apply to any worthwhile project, which would remove their money from going into a large black hole that presently governments create.

The taxpayer would see that they had contributed to something beneficial to their community. The list of benefits to industry would grow, as investment to our future is essential.

A new and fresh outlook and way of thinking will take us into a new dynamic future, where each of us feels that we have a part to play. Individually, we would have a more meaningful contribution to give to a society that shares more equally with its people than ever before.

Education

The word 'education' will mean just that, educating children to develop the skills and gifts that they possess. Furthermore, it would be vital to show each child that they have an equal and important part to play in this new society. Each young person needs to be taught that their role whether it be looking after the elderly, or keeping the streets tidy, is just as important as a child who excels academically. Whilst academic ability is important, so are many of the jobs in society that are considered to be more mundane. As a society we fail to teach children that they are all individuals capable of so many things of varying degrees of ability.

Schools need to develop the natural attributes that some children possess that may not be regarded as academic. For instance, it may be cooking, caring, horticultural tendencies, in fact, the list could go on forever. We must have places to develop these gifts and abilities from an early stage, maybe from the age of twelve. Once children have learned the foundation of the three Rs by the age of twelve, then it is time to educate and train them in their natural gifts and attributes.

For example, nursing could be a natural attribute that could be nurtured at such an age, along with many other professions, which could become apprenticeships when they reach 18 years old. Through careful planning, organisation, and vision, we could meet all the demand of jobs in each and every profession. Therefore, jobs would be waiting, as we would not be pulling skilled people from other countries, who cannot afford to lose such people themselves. Our future depends upon the children of the present, yet as a society we are failing them in so many ways.

Furthermore, we are failing our children in not being able to create sufficient outside activities and interests after school hours for them. This is an important factor, because children need other pursuits beside school itself in order to maintain happiness and a sense of balance in their life. The list of worthwhile pursuits for our youngsters could be extensive, but such things are not considered as some of them are allowed to vegetate in an aimless existence. Such ones are then in a danger of drifting into crime, due to the inequalities within our society.

Therefore, as a society, we must help children to progress and believe in their own abilities and gifts. This, in turn, installs them with self-confidence, helping them to pursue a job that fulfils their heart rather than their pocket. In other words, they would be much happier performing a job that suits their natural abilities, rather than putting the burden of material pursuit on their career decision. We need to help those who are in circumstances where they have no loving home to go to, or are suffering in other deprived areas of social background.

The whole ethos of teaching and evaluating our children needs to be changed. Such change needs to be lead by example, and the belief that everyone can lead a more fulfilled and satisfying life. There is no easy way to do this and there are no short cuts, but there is a better way than the one at present. Our present methods are failing and have constantly failed, as the evidence has clearly portrayed. We must remove the myth that the main goal in life is to have a job that pays high monetary returns. A well-paid job does not result in happiness; rather, fulfilment and job satisfaction comes before money.

This is the essence behind the message of change; it is better to give than to receive. All controls of education policy must be by the government creating many types of academy schools under a larger umbrella of thinking. There needs to be academies for every sort of trade and career; ranging from house building and gardening to the dentist, chemist, scientist, and shop assistant.

Consequently, everyone will discover a role that suits them. No private funding, which enables private companies to profit out of their activity, will be allowed to operate such a venture. Rather, the new pillars of society will stand by the efforts and principles of everyone, without one benefiting at the cost of another.

Students at University

The present situation that places so many students in debt in order to obtain their degrees for whatever profession, or purpose they pursue, is wrong. It appears to be widely accepted that a person should begin their career with debt. However, this situation in its very essence is morally wrong, and should not be an acceptable situation.

To nurture the ability of people and give them the best education we can offer, should not come at a price of starting working life with a huge debt hanging over them. Make no mistake; funding can be achieved in other ways and means. For instance, we could start by scrapping the proposed £35 billion due to be spent on re-equipping nuclear submarines.

We could prevent students from applying for university if they are just viewing it as an "easy ride". A course of action could be implemented if a student failed after the first year. Maybe, for example, paying the equivalent to that year's tuition.

Moreover, if a student emigrated within the first five years of their career after graduation, then they would be required to pay for each year's fees that they had fallen short of the required five years. For example, if they emigrated after four years of their career, they would be required to pay a year's fees for their degree.

Such a fresh approach would help everyone in the long term, because as a country we are the beneficiaries. Indeed, as a country now, we are calculating the various shortages and needs in the future requirements of building the foundations of a better and more fulfilled society.

Foreign Affairs

It has always been important where we stand in the world with others, as our country has played a big part in the shaping and making of other countries. There will be many countries we will agree with, where history has formed bonds of friendship and alliances have remained strong. With any foreign policy it is making further friends and giving help when necessary to those who feel they have a great deal in common with us.

Therefore, our judgement must always be what we feel is right for us. We have to lead and set examples to others if we are to gain respect. The way forward in the coming years will see great changes and it will be this country that will lead by example. We need to have an independent mind even if we are at odds with others. We have given a lot to others in the past, and will continue to do so. By being confident and believing we can create a better future, it is hoped others can follow our example of creating a society that removes injustices, giving greater opportunity and freedom to all.

Banks

Changes must be made in the way that banks operate. They have fuelled a culture of borrowing by dropping the standards that they once had. To push money at the vulnerable, encouraging people to take on debt that they can ill afford, is equal to supplying more alcohol to someone who is already struggling with a drink problem. It is equally immoral for banks and others who entice people into believing there is no problem in borrowing. To lend money to anyone knowing that they can ill afford to take on such loans, speaks volumes of where we have sunk to as a society. The banks know no depths to which they will sink to, just in the pursuit of profit. If a profit has to be found at the misfortune of another, this says exactly what we have resorted to as a society and where we are now.

No government leadership illustrates why, as a country, we are bankrupt. As a country we are bankrupt of morals, values, ideas, and deeply in debt. Building societies and banks are fuelling an inevitable crash with homes. By changing their previous standards of giving mortgages, we now see young people borrowing more and more all the time. By allowing such a flood of money, the consequences will be dire. With the stress, worry, depression and despair which is associated with debt, what sort of society are we creating? The banks can sit equally with anyone when it comes to creating broken families, divorces, ill health, and even tragedies with some people.

Therefore, an ethical code of banking practices and standards are urgently required, with government also governing with such ethical practices and standards.

Utilities and Energy

Water must come under the umbrella of government. To have such an essential asset in the control of private companies operating for profit is abhorrent. Just because previous governments have failed to invest and maintain the structures of the water system does not mean a competent government cannot do the job.

We have to plan and think further ahead for our future generations. We need to put plans into action that will be efficient and lasting. With all our energy resources we have to be in unison with planning and investing into new technology, which will lead to other sources of energy. We also need to think of as many ways as possible to save energy. We now have to be focused and conscious that energy resources have to be regarded as the crown jewels to the future of our very existence. We have to think of better ways of heating our homes, building all houses that comply with such thinking.

Nuclear energy must disappear along with the dinosaur thinking of holding nuclear weapons. For any prospect of life for future generations, the nuclear option must disappear. The power of the future will be hydropower, and we, like others, have to invest heavily in order to bring about this new energy that will power cars and play such an important role for the future. Change in how we think and perceive the future must begin by removing the boundaries of thought.

Transport Policy

We have never had a coherent transport policy. We have never had anyone with vision of what our requirements and needs are for the future. Government must have control of railways and all our major transport facilities so that plans can be implemented which look beyond a five-year period. We should have built motorways twice the size to accommodate a motorway just for heavy-goods vehicles, and one parallel for family/smaller traffic. How on earth can we plan and create what is required when we have so many companies with different agendas, but the one linking them is profit.

To create a system that removes a number of cars from our roads, we have to accept that travel is a necessity, and we have to think differently as our over-populated island is already ceasing to function. We need to create a railway system that is capable of carrying more passengers at a minimal cost, making it cheaper and quicker than using cars. All trains could be double-decker travel with more routes available.

To travel by car for each individual is already showing the impossibility of continuing with this existing policy. With better motorways, bus transport, and the use of double-deckers, would have a greater impact and prove cheaper and more efficient than cars.

We could eventually do away with cars if we provide a different and better alternative means of travel; cheaper trains, more rail track, larger and more efficient tube systems in London and other main city problem areas etc. A profit on travel would only exist to provide further investment into the travel system.

Again, it is government that has to be in control for planning, investments, and long-term strategies. It always amazes so many people why all the road tax collected is not fully reinvested in creating a worthwhile transport system. Again, like with so many other things, it is the blind leading the blind.

Defence

A strong military force has always been a requirement. The defence of one's country and to fight for democracy, has stood for years. However, surely the amount of money spent on armour around the world is a terrible waste of resources. The barrel of a gun will not achieve peace and reconciliation around the world. With all the conflicts that exist, you have to ask why the different ideologies, cultures, viewpoints, injustices, all expressions that are feeding hate and oppression, and in some case, tyranny. With all of this you can see a combustion of flames that will spread. You cannot put out one fire and leave another to burn. With so many that are fuelled by others whose grievances are similar, if not the same, as their own. You have to listen, understand the other viewpoint, and go down the road from where the feelings fan the flames. Brute force and weaponry is not the answer.

The action that will bring peace about is one of the greatest gifts we possess, and it is called 'giving'. Not just giving by some, but giving by all. With each fire that burns, the injustices of the past have to be swept away. By going down this road all problems that are man-made can be resolved by giving. If one believes that giving to a perceived adversary is a sign of weakness, then the opposite is true. It is strength that has brought you to that decision and position. If the so-called adversary lays down all his encumbrances, we then listen and try to understand their point of view. This is giving, just listening. Remember, with some the fire will be ferocious. By giving with perseverance eventually the flame will subside because you are allowing all the heat to emit. So, problems rest with the action of evil, but even this force can be disarmed.

Agriculture

As a country we need to be self-sufficient in almost all departments of commerce, industry, and farming. We cannot allow farms to go to the wall because supermarkets are able to dictate with their global purchasing power. If we look at the plight of the dairy industry, by putting extreme pressures on milk prices, we could see a situation where milk in bigger quantities is purchased abroad. We would then see the demise of further farms. We need to have a bigger plan of where our food comes from. With warmer climates we are already seeing produce being grown which we would not have associated with our climate. With food being an essential commodity, we have to think further into the future, for other countries, with help, could adopt the same policy. Farms will inevitably form bigger groups. Crops will be grown in specific areas, which are more beneficial. Consequently, we have to manage land in a far better way. Smaller farms, however, will probably have to merge with others in order to increase efficiency. Certain areas will only accommodate sheep etc. By managing the land we can keep prices probably relative to what it would have cost to import such goods.

Those generations who have tilled the land could pay an important part with their expertise in utilising their abilities, which harness their fulfilment of working with animals and the land.

By keeping our focus on the future, we will not allow global companies to dictate the strategy of the country, which will enable the government to govern and create a better life for all, not just the few.

Youth Programme

We need all youngsters contributing a minimum of twelve months in the youth corps where they would live within a camp of military disciplines. Here, a plan of action would involve all working within their community to give their time in one project or another. By giving, they will learn that nothing in life comes without a cost. But, more importantly, the realisation that it is their community and that they can be involved with it.

Work would be provided that would suit the natural abilities of the youngsters, rather than throwing them into something that they would hate. It would be something that they would feel fulfilling and worthwhile in doing. As a result, they would feel proud of whatever they achieved as an individual, and a team. By uniting the best attributes of the youngsters, it would be a positive action that would help them to believe in themselves and each other. It would nurture a camaraderie that will take their friendships throughout life.

All of this may appear idealistic, but it is achievable. We must cultivate the aspirations of the young if we want a better future. It would be an important platform to give them confidence in their own abilities, which would probably never have been found, unless we encourage them that they each have something valuable to give. The age of sixteen is a pivotal stage in their development, and it is at such an age that it is vital to harness their energy in the pursuit of good, positive, goals in life.

Law and Order

The order of a society is determined by its own values, principles, morals, standards, attitudes, and thoughts. If a society encourages a material-led existence then it has a powerful impact upon the way that their population lead their life, and as a consequence, they mirror the standards of the society that they live in. It is this ill-made recipe that regurgitates the pain and problems, one could metaphorically say continuing stomachaches, and until its symptoms are fully diagnosed, the patient will continue to decline with the inevitable consequences.

By having an economy that is based on the sovereignty of consumer spending, we have created a one-way autobahn that is leading us in the wrong direction. Like any tree that has grown, we have to tackle the root of the problem.

The law, which we have at present, is flawed in so many ways due to the symptoms that have already been discussed. The question is, are we administering the right cure? No. It has been quoted that we spend £100,000 per prisoner to provide a lock-up facility for offenders. This is an abhorrent use of public money. Prison facilities could be self-sustaining, and each prisoner could, if they overcome the cause of their wrong ways, be trained in various capacities to be of value to him/herself and their community. Failure in changing their ways would see such prisoners having to live and sustain themselves in an environment that would not encourage a long-term accommodation.

The present practice of locking someone up for twenty-three hours a day is inhumane, and there is nothing to be gained from the individual. We then release such ones without a trade or place of employment. Therefore, we see the perpetuation of the same crime committed time and again. This is the surreal situation we ourselves have created. Therefore, we would offer freedom and the chance of redemption, in the knowledge that further help is available, as the prize to gain at the end of their sentence.

It is only through change and new foundations that we can try to eliminate the present increasing rate in crime.

Welfare and Benefits

The present regime of giving with nothing being given back is unpalatable, and we are perpetuating a culture that will never harvest a crop from which we can benefit from. I can speak from first hand experience, where circumstances saw me raising four daughters (10, 12, 15, 17) and not having £5 to my name. Living in a dilapidated caravan, the system allowed me to be there and succeed in three of my daughters reaching university. If I'd have had a job I would have failed, I had to take into account severe pain with my arthritis. Therefore, everything is not wrong. Circumstance is the criteria then. I could, at a later date teach art and design as this is one of my abilities. Society, however, does not accommodate the use of such abilities and qualities that could help the young. We try to fit people into boxes that many will not accept and those boxes have been created by the job market. The big difference is that we need to be the one to decide where we feel that we fit into the picture, effectively making 'the box' for our personal preferences. It is no good placing someone whose ability is accountancy, into being a robot that what would be for them, some soul-destroying job.

Society needs to recognise and harness the vast amount of knowledge and abilities each and every one of us has gained through life experience. The person who believes they have failed can help others not to make what may have been elementary mistakes. Each person has something to give; society just needs to find a way of utilising this wealth of experience and employing it in the right way. By viewing abilities in a different way and creating new jobs, which won't be viewed as 'work', we could see a new dawn in the whole concept of employment. Who better to teach the wrongdoing youngsters of the error of their ways than someone who has spent years in jail and realises the consequences of such behaviour?

We have to create a new view and culture of thinking. For instance, those who carry disabilities but have abilities of communication could become mentors to those who find themselves in a place of despair. Furthermore, the one who has overcome alcoholism could give precious help and guidance to those who are suffering with addictions of their own. One could keep going on with such examples, but the main thing is to bear in mind that such new ways of thinking are part of the new building blocks required to help society advance.

The culture that our society is helping to promote young mothers has to be curtailed. They are encouraged to have more children because our government appears to reward them through state benefits. Also, the fathers seem to be out of the picture totally quite often. This also needs to change. So, those males who encourage larger families, but evade any responsibility, would have appropriate jobs found for them.

By rebuilding these present foundations all people would benefit, especially those who live in a box that does not allow the best to grow within them. A new meaning and purpose will see all realms of society prospering in a way never seen before. We will value everyone and those who need help. Imagine a society where no one is left unfulfilled.

Immigration

Immigration on the present scale is unsustainable. To provide validity by offering the argument that it is advantageous to the economy is a fallacy. No one has given a figure that equates to one million entering the country on the cost to social services, i.e. schooling, health, welfare, housing, and countless other costs which simultaneously appear. Add this additional cost and one can simply see that we cannot sustain, or even provide a fraction of the cost without a disadvantage to our home-born population, who are already in a hopeless position of trying to find, or obtain, a home of their own. We are already in meltdown and we are in surreal times that are hard to cope with.

One cannot blame people who migrate to this country, especially those from countries that are in dire circumstances, or those who try to provide a better life for their families. The answer to this problem is stark, but real. We cannot accept anymore, we have to overrule, if not abandon, any such further thoughts of allowing in anymore. We need to allow those now that have entered only a limited work time and try to provide the answers and actions to address home affairs.

There is only one answer to the migration of so many around the world. We have to help and give the necessary building blocks that encourage each country to have hope and faith that a better future exists for them as it does for us. As we create new foundations we could act as a model for others.

The corrupt and tyrannical regimes have to be removed for the sake of the majority, so that everyone can help to build their country in a way that benefits the whole. Sanctuary will have to be provided for the extreme cases, but equally, all must share it.

Man can eradicate the famines and poverty that regularly occur if they unite with the strong helping the weak. New building blocks have to be placed for those countries that, for many, still exist in a by-gone age. It will take years, but to continue with present policies illustrates progress is minimal. To give money to those who need to build, is equal to giving money and materials to build a home, when none are qualified to build such a home.

We have got to provide all the necessary infrastructure and administration of a democratic government, which will take a generation to complete before one could successfully hand over the reins of governing. Numerous government structures such as health, education, etc, would have to be fully competent to administer and govern.

The world as it is has to change to bring balance and help to others, whilst eliminating the many injustices that still continue for so many.

Health

As a country we can say, and this applies to everyone, 'Health is your Wealth'. If we look to the N.H.S as though this institution is the panacea to all our ills; well, this is not the case. It is a help, but not the cure or answer to our health. More times than not our health is determined by how we conduct our life. This can be helped if we understand the meaning and purpose to our life.

A priority is the improvement to the N.H.S. to help it become more efficient so that it carries on helping and healing people. We need to have sufficient staff, i.e. nurses, doctors, surgeons, technicians, consultants, dentists etc, which come under the same umbrella, and all other ancillary staff. This staff needs to be drawn from our own country. To have doctors etc. bringing their skills for the lure of money from countries, which in many cases are impoverished and urgently require those skills, is morally wrong. Again, we have to plan to train and fill such vacancies ourselves. We have to remove the bureaucracy that has no conception of our requirements for the future. This failure, though, lies with governments who have been blind to the needs of our society. Let those who have posed the question that our health services along with others would have collapsed without foreign workers answer the question. We have failed to manage and have any vision to the needs of our country.

The biggest flaw to the N.H.S. is again at the step of government. We have created a society of robots, whom have lost their way in knowing how to eat right, and no longer know the meaning of their life. This illustrates that the present structures have been wrong in virtually every way. We are reaping what we have sown – drink, drugs, money, materialism, and selfishness. The idolatry of so many false idols, i.e. the celebrity culture, of so many sad people. The list goes on and on, and we are all part of this vehicle that has been running on the wrong track. Now, more than ever, we can see the inevitability of the wheels, one by one, falling off. Change is not just part of the whole, it is needed to completely make a new start that will lay down the foundations for future generations.

We will have the necessary academies to train the dentists and nurses alike. We could also bring many people, who have been stigmatised by age, to give help by being there with patients, and providing further help to those who are in need. The care for those who are in the winter of their life should have the best care available. The present circumstances of care homes being run as a profit would go forever. To profit out of the aged and infirmed is abhorrent, and for those who have worked all their lives and been forced to sell their homes is morally wrong. We are all responsible for the elderly in our society.

There are so many areas where more funding is required, i.e. mental health etc., but in the long term when people begin to see their own true value, and meaning to life, all will change. So much of ill health is caused by the way that society has created, in many ways, its own hell. The strength of our own spirit will open the appropriate doors to breathe new life into everyone.

These thoughts and suggestions are all possible and feasible if we unite as a nation. It is time for change NOW.

This is just the bones of the New Foundations required. The flesh will be added when people believe we can have a better society and have a new view of what life is truly about.